# Storing Food

Written by Ann-Marie Parker

## CONTENTS

# Why Do Animals Store Food?

In the amazing world of animals, there are many ways that animals store food. Some animals store it so they can survive winter when food is hard to find. Other animals store food to feed their young. Animals have lots of unusual places to store their food.

Why do animals store food?

- To have enough food to eat in winter.

- To feed their babies.

- To protect their food so others won't get it.

- So that they can survive long journeys.

# Storing Food for Winter

In winter, animals find it harder to get food. Some plants do not grow well in the ground when it is cold. Animals need to store food in the summer months so they have enough to eat in winter.

## Beavers

Beavers store branches and twigs deep in the water so they can eat them later. They anchor the branches under the water near their lodges in areas called caches. During winter, they swim from their lodges, under the water and ice, to eat the bark on branches they stored.

# Squirrels

In places where it is very hot in summer and cold in winter, squirrels store food. They gather as many seeds and nuts as they can in the summer when they grow well. The squirrels then store the food in holes in the ground.

Squirrels hide their food:

- under fallen leaves
- in holes in the ground
- near their nests so they can protect it from other animals.

Once winter has arrived, the squirrels need to find where they have stored their food. A squirrel must have a very good sense of smell and a very good memory. Otherwise, all that work would have been for nothing.

# Storing Food for Others

Ants and bees are very good at storing food in their hives or nests. The stored food is used for feeding babies and adults.

## Bees

Honey bees live in hives where food is stored in the honeycomb. Worker bees collect pollen and honey and store it in cells in the honeycomb. The pollen and honey is used later to feed other bees in the hive. Some cells in the honeycomb have eggs in them.

Honeycomb is made out of wax from the bees' bodies.

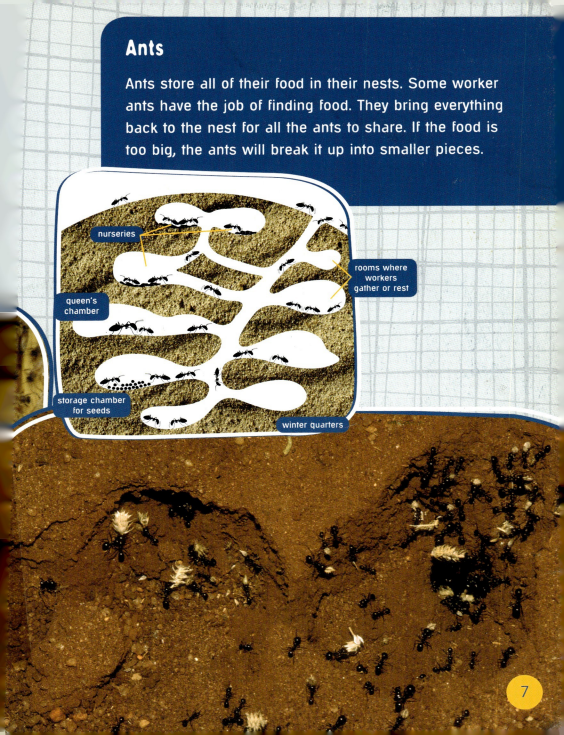

# Ants

Ants store all of their food in their nests. Some worker ants have the job of finding food. They bring everything back to the nest for all the ants to share. If the food is too big, the ants will break it up into smaller pieces.

nurseries

rooms where workers gather or rest

queen's chamber

storage chamber for seeds

winter quarters

# Animals That Store Fat

Some animals store fat in their bodies, which they can use for energy at a later time.

## Bears

Before winter comes and it is hard to find food, bears eat as much food as they can. Then they find a place to sleep for the winter. While they are sleeping and dozing, the bears are able to use the fat they have stored in their bodies.

## Camels

Camels are able to store fat in their humps. This fat is later burned by the camel's body for energy. The camel needs energy on long journeys through the desert.

Some people think that a camel stores water in its hump. There is only fat in a camel's hump. But camels can travel long distances without water. When they do find water, they can drink a huge amount at one time.

## Male Emperor Penguins

A father penguin needs to be able to survive without food for up to 64 days while the mother penguin goes in search of food. During this time, the father penguin lives off the fat he has stored in his body. When the mother penguin returns to feed the chick, the father penguin can then go hunting for food.

# Storing Food Underground

Chipmunks and hamsters keep their food under the ground. Storing food in tunnels or burrows under the ground means they can get to it quickly and easily and protect it from other animals.

## Hamsters

Some types of hamsters live by themselves and only come out at night. Hamsters are very good at digging burrows. They have different parts of the burrow for different things. In a hamster burrow, there is a part for nesting, a part for food storage and a place for body wastes.

A hamster in its nest.

## Chipmunks

Chipmunks sleep through a lot of winter. If a chipmunk needs food, it will wake up and eat the food that it has stored in its tunnel. Once it has had some seeds and nuts, it can go back to sleep again.

# Storing Food in Stomachs

Looking after hungry baby animals can be a lot of work. These animals have a very different way of storing food for their babies.

## Penguins

When the mother penguin returns, she feeds her chick from the food in her crop. The crop looks like a sack and is the first part of her stomach. The mother penguin brings up the food bit by bit from her crop into her throat. This makes it easier for the chick to get to the food.

## Wolves

Young cubs are cared for in dens. When they are ready to eat food, their mother and younger brothers and sisters help feed them. Baby cubs are fed meat that hasn't been digested properly. The meat is regurgitated for them to eat. This gives the baby cubs all the food they need until they can hunt for themselves.

# Unusual Ways of Storing Food

## Food for Later

A spider can wrap up its dinner and eat it later. It does this by wrapping up an insect in its silky web. There is no way that the insect can get free. The spider does not have to worry about its dinner running away.

banded garden spider

leafcutter ants

## Storing Food That Can Grow

The leafcutter ant got its name because it cuts up pieces of leaf and brings them back to its nest. Once the ant is back in its nest, it chews the leaves into little pieces. The ant then grows tiny fungi on the leaves. This white fungi is good food to eat and to feed their babies.

white fungi

# Humans Store Food, Too

Long ago, humans found ways of keeping their food from going bad. During winter, they would keep their food outside where it would stay cold. During summer, they would find somewhere cool, like a cave, to keep their food cold. Food was stored so that it could be used later when it was hard to find food.

Today, we have lots of different ways to store food in our homes. We can store food in the fridge or freezer to keep it cold. And we can store it in jars or containers. This keeps the air out so that it stays as fresh as possible.

Here are some ways of storing food so it will last for a longer time:

- in the fridge
- in the freezer
- in cans
- in bottles and jars.

# Index

# Reports

## Storing Food is a Report

**A report has a topic:**

### Storing Food

**A report has headings:**

### Why Do Animals Store Food?

### Storing Food for Winter?

### Storing Food for Others

Some information is put under headings.

### Unusual Ways of Storing Food

- Spiders wrap up their food.
- Leafcutter ants grow their food.

Information can be shown in other ways.

This report has . . .

**Labels**  **Photographs**

**Captions**  **Bullet points**

**Cross-section diagram**

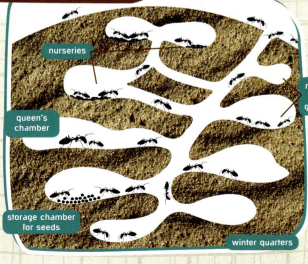

nurseries

rooms where workers gather or rest

queen's chamber

storage chamber for seeds

winter quarters

# Guide Notes

> **Title: Storing Food**
> **Stage:** Fluency
>
> **Text Form:** Informational Report
> **Approach:** Guided Reading
> **Processes:** Thinking Critically, Exploring Language, Processing Information
> **Written and Visual Focus:** Contents Page, Labels, Captions, Index, Bullet Points,
> Cross-section Diagram

## THINKING CRITICALLY
(sample questions)

### Before Reading – Establishing Prior Knowledge
• What do you know about storing food?

### Visualising the Text Content
• What might you expect to see in this book?
• What form of writing do you think will be used by the author?
Look at the contents page and index. Encourage the students to think about the information and make predictions about the text content.

### After Reading – Interpreting the Text
• What would it be like if you had to store all the food you needed for winter?
• Why is storing food important? Why do you think that?
• Why do you think some animals store food and other animals don't?
• Why is storing food important to people? In what ways do you store food?
• What do you know about storing food that you didn't know before?
• What things in the book helped you to understand the information?
• What questions do you have after reading the text?

## EXPLORING LANGUAGE

### Terminology
Photograph credits, index, contents page, imprint information, ISBN number